It Will Not Quit

by Lauren Quillin
illustrated by Amanda Harvey

Practice Decodable 48

McGraw Hill Education

Bothell, WA • Chicago, IL • Columbus, OH • New York, NY

MHEonline.com

Send all inquiries to:
McGraw-Hill Education
8787 Orion Place
Columbus, OH 43240

ISBN: 978-0-02-138912-4
MHID: 0-02-138912-8

Printed in China.

8 9 10 11 12 DSS 27 26 25 24 23

Jill and Jess sat.

Jill had my quilt on her lap.

"Summer has ended," said Jess.

A quick squirrel grabbed a nut.

"A squirrel's job is to gather nuts.
Squirrels will not quit," said Jill.

Bugs buzzed past Jill.
"Quit bugging us!" she said.

Jill ducked under the quilt.
Jess grinned.

"A bug's job is to bug!" said Jess.
"It will not quit."